P9-CLE-193

20

Kansas City, MO Public Library

0000187877675

FOR MY EDITOR, CAROL HINZ, WHO SPOTTED THIS STORY
FIRST—AND SAW IT CLEARLY EVEN WHEN I COULDN'T

—C.B.

FOR MY MOM, WHO SOMEHOW HAS ALWAYS
MANAGED TO SEE MY QUIRKS AS GIFTS.
THANK YOU FOR GIVING ME THE COURAGE TO BE DIFFERENT.

—V.N.

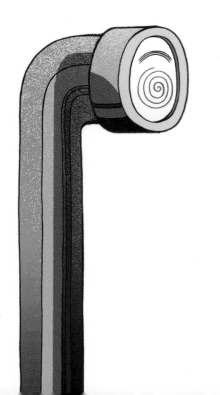

DAZZLE SHIPS

WORLD WAR I and the ART of CONFUSION

CHRIS BARTON

illustrated by VICTO NGAI

M MILLBROOK PRESS • MINNEAPOLIS

NOTE: *England is the largest country in the United Kingdom, which is abbreviated UK and is also informally known as Britain. The UK ran the British Empire, which included people and territories all over the world. And it was the UK's Royal Navy that made that empire possible. The British Empire was one of the major participants in World War I, which lasted from 1914 to 1918 and was known at the time as the Great War. The British allied with (among others) Russia, France, Italy, Serbia, Romania and, starting in 1917, the United States to fight mainly Germany, Austria-Hungary, and the Ottoman Empire.*

WORLD

ONE OF THE SHIPS ON THIS PAGE IS PAINTED IN SNEAKY, STRIPY CAMOUFLAGE.

You probably can't even see it.

Oh. You *can* see it?

Hmmmmmmm.

That ship was an allied vessel used during World War I, and it was camouflaged so strangely for a reason.

More than 1,200 US ships were decked out that way, and so were more than twice as many ships in the British fleet. The idea was to make these ships harder for German torpedoes to sink.

World War I, which lasted from 1914 to 1918, was one of the largest wars the world had seen. Many nations were involved, including Germany on one side and the United Kingdom (and, eventually, the United States) on the other.

UNITED

KINGDOM

FRANCE

German submarines, known as U-boats, were attacking—and sinking—ships in Britain's Royal Navy. (The *U* stood for *Unterseeboot*, or undersea boat.) They were also sinking other ships carrying all kinds of things, including food. As an island nation, Britain depended on goods arriving by sea. Too few boats were reaching Britain, and food was running out. The country might have to surrender so its people could eat.

Submarines and the torpedoes they fired were big changes in the way wars were fought. Never before could an enemy hide beneath the waves and attack from a mile away. A U-boat crew would use its periscope to quickly peek above the surface of the water, pick a target, and launch a torpedo toward the spot where its target was going to be in a minute or so. Torpedoes were slower back then, but they were deadly.

The sinking of ships—especially non-fighting ships—
without any warning was new too. In the early years
of the war, Germany limited which ships its U-boats
attacked. But in early 1917, it saw a chance to win
the war by starving Britain, its strongest opponent.

Britain tried different things to stop the submarine attacks. There was talk of training seagulls and sea lions to spot the subs and of having swimmers smash U-boats' periscopes with hammers. The British started having their supply ships stick close together and sail in convoys guarded by armed vessels. The Royal Navy began using depth charges—three-hundred-pound underwater weapons that would explode when they sank to certain levels—to damage or destroy U-boats.

CONVOYS PLAN

TOP-SECRET

DEPTH CHARGE

Mark II

Thrower

U-BOAT

fig. 1

And a Royal Naval Volunteer Reserve lieutenant-commander named Norman Wilkinson had another suggestion. It was unlikely. It was improbable. It may have even seemed bonkers. His idea was to camouflage the ships.

Wilkinson's responsibilities included patrolling the waters off southwestern England and sweeping for mines. He saw a lot of ships as part of his job. One Monday morning, after a weekend away spent fishing, he was headed back to work when inspiration struck.

"I suddenly got the idea that since it was impossible to paint a ship so that she could not be seen by a submarine, the extreme opposite was the answer—to paint her, not for low visibility, but in such a way as to break up her form and thus confuse a submarine officer as to the course on which she was heading."

The word *camouflage* itself was brand-new at the time. But the concept of camouflage—of fooling an enemy into seeing something other than what's actually there—was an old one.

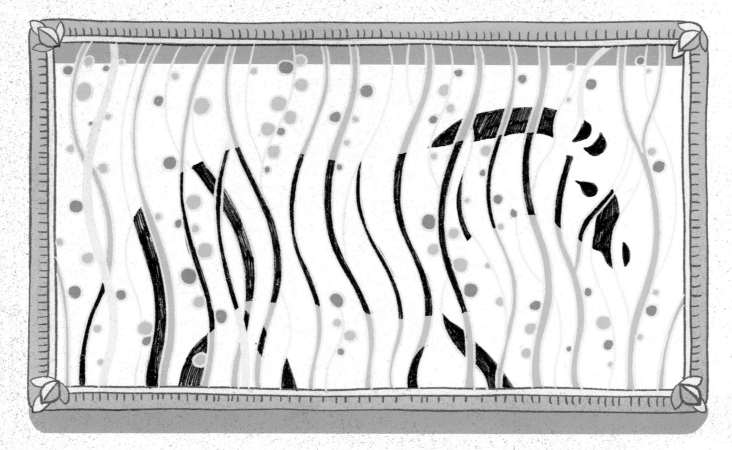

And Wilkinson wasn't the first person ever to suggest camouflage for ships. Imaginative folks in the fields of art and science had tried before.

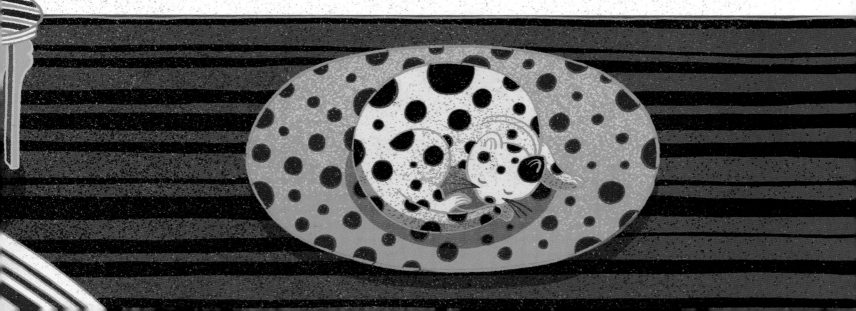

Wilkinson, however, got his idea at just the right time. The British government was desperate to stop the U-boat attacks. It listened to Wilkinson's plan, named his approach "**DAZZLE**," and said (more or less), "**Give it a try!**"

So he did. In spring 1917, he had a ship dazzle-painted with a crazy-looking pattern on one side and a crazy-looking pattern on the other side. These patterns were supposed to confuse German submarine crews about the ships' direction and speed.

Dazzle was meant to make the Germans think a ship was, for example, turning toward the west when it was actually headed to the southeast.

U-boats didn't carry many torpedoes. If dazzle could cause a German sub to waste a torpedo by firing it to a spot where a British ship wasn't actually going to be—and if this happened over and over—then more British ships would stay afloat and get their cargo to their destination.

fore
side

aft
side

length 410'

The Royal Navy liked Wilkinson's first ship, so it asked
for fifty more done up in dazzle. And it liked those
next fifty so much that it asked him to paint every
stuff-carrying ship that Britain had with those
crazy combinations of black, white, gray,
green, blue, purple, and pink.

Of course, Wilkinson couldn't do all this on his own. Two dozen young
women who had been to art schools did a lot of the work. They
painted designs onto wooden models, and then they copied the best
designs onto paper. Each approved dazzle design got rushed off to ports
all over England where painters—laborers and artists alike—applied
them to the sides of ships that were being unloaded and reloaded.

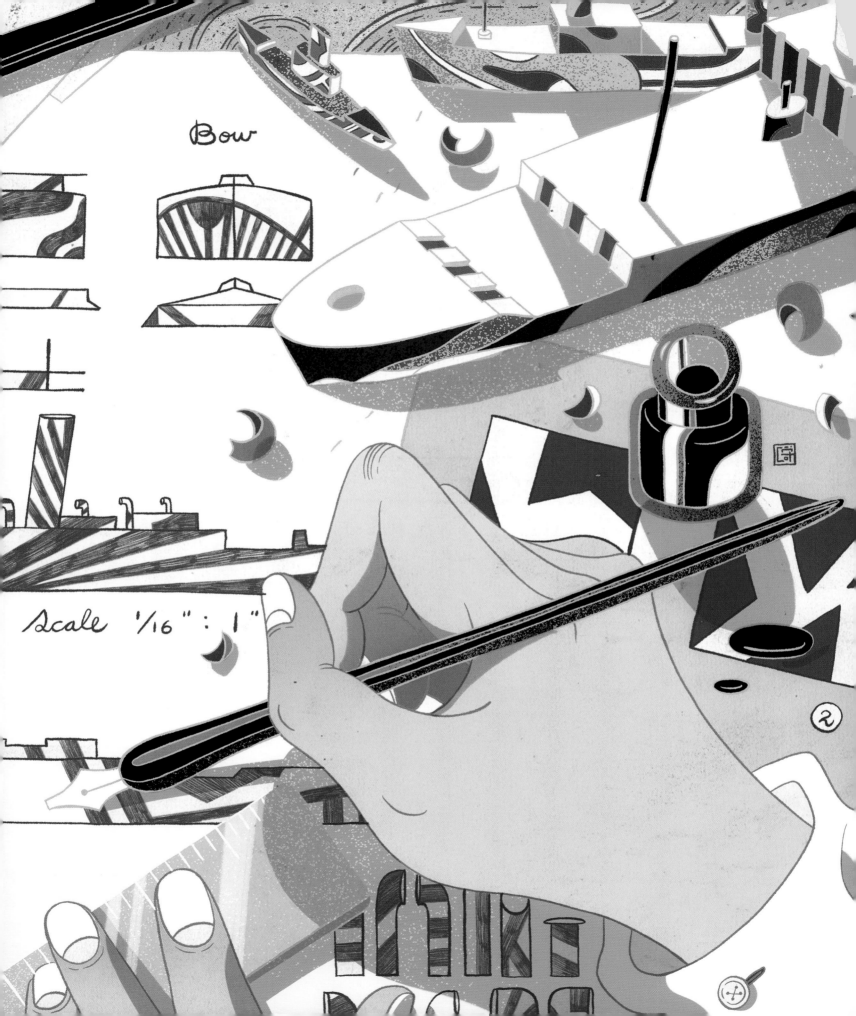

How did Wilkinson know which designs to use? He had a test. One day, the king of the United Kingdom dropped by to have a look.

Now, King George V knew a lot about ships, because he had joined the Royal Navy when he was just twelve years old. Wilkinson had the king look through a submarine periscope at a painted model on a rotating table. All the king had to do was figure out which direction the model ship was pointed in. It took him a while—more time than a sub commander would have had—but finally the king had his answer.

SOUTH BY WEST,
decided the king.

Actually, Wilkinson replied,
the model was pointing
EAST-SOUTHEAST.

King George V had just been told that he was wrong. His Majesty walked over to the model for a closer look.

"Commander," he supposedly said to Wilkinson, "I have been a professional sailor for many years and I would not have believed I could have been so deceived in my estimate."

In other words, the king himself had been . . . **DAZZLED**.

Britain wasn't the only country doing the dazzling. After the United States entered the war, it went for dazzle in a big way. It even used dazzle to draw attention to a ship-shaped New York City naval recruiting station.

Members of the Women's Reserve Camouflage Corps did the painting overnight, surprising those who had walked past a gray-colored building just the evening before.

Britain, the United States, and their allies turned things around, and Germany surrendered in November 1918. By the time the fighting stopped, 1,256 American ships had been painted in dazzle designs along with close to 3,000 British ships.

So just how well did dazzle work? Nobody really knows. The U-boat attacks stopped succeeding, but historians mostly give the credit to convoys and depth charges. (Sorry, sea lions.)

While the United States said right after the war that dazzle kept lots of ships from getting sunk, Britain wasn't so sure. The Royal Navy couldn't prove that dazzle had actually spared any ships. But some insisted that at the very least, the sailors on those ships just felt better knowing that something had been tried to keep them from getting torpedoed.

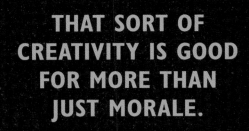

THAT SORT OF CREATIVITY IS GOOD FOR MORE THAN JUST MORALE.

Times change.
Technology changes.
Torpedoes get faster,
submarine targeting
systems get computerized,
challenges of all kinds get
replaced by new ones.
But a willingness to tackle
problems by trying the
unlikely, the improbable,
the seemingly bonkers will
always be needed.

After all, as those of
us inspired by Norman
Wilkinson's paint job
know, sometimes
desperate times call for
DAZZLING measures.

AUTHOR'S NOTE

Dazzle camouflage is a real-life example of information overload. When used on ships during World War I, those colors and patterns served as extra information that made it hard to figure out which way a ship was heading. Likewise, research for a nonfiction book sometimes turns up extra information that can make it hard to determine which way the story should go.

This book began when editor Carol Hinz suggested I listen to an episode about dazzle ships from the podcast *99% Invisible*, saying "It brings together art, design, and military history in a really interesting way."

I listened, and I liked what I heard. So I got a couple of books from the library: Peter Forbes's *Dazzled and Deceived: Mimicry and Camouflage* and Nicholas Rankin's *A Genius for Deception: How Cunning Helped the British Win Two World Wars*.

Luckily for me, the authors of those first two books listed the books that they had learned from. This is pretty typical of how my nonfiction research works: I have a question (what are dazzle ships?), I find out who can answer that question, then I find out who answered their questions, and from there I keep on working my way backward.

I also worked my way outward into subjects such as torpedo speed, the origin of the word *camouflage*, and a short-lived style of art known as vorticism. I came across the names of many notable people (and one famous ship) along the way, and while King George V made it through my many revisions, I ultimately left out Theodore Roosevelt, Winston Churchill, Arthur Conan Doyle, Gertrude Stein, Pablo Picasso, and the *Titanic*.

Focusing on the famous can be fun, but none of those names are as important to the story as Norman Wilkinson's name. To keep the story streamlined, I left them out. And even a couple of genuinely significant names failed to make the cut.

Painter Abbott Handerson Thayer (1849–1921) loved creating portraits of women with angel wings, but it was his observations of other subjects that gave him strong opinions about how animals' skin, feathers, and fur protect them from predators. He believed that animals with "ruptive" patterns—sharply contrasting colors side by side—were harder to recognize. And he thought ruptive patterns could benefit ships as well.

Scientist John Graham Kerr (1869–1957) studied the South American lungfish. He also had ideas for painting ships to make them less visible, using contrasting colors to make their edges harder to see.

But the Royal Navy didn't pay much attention to either Thayer's ideas or Kerr's. Wilkinson wasn't pushy and full of himself like Thayer, and he had better connections than Kerr. As a result, he was more successful at getting the people in charge of the Royal Navy to take him seriously—and to provide the help he needed to carry out his plan.

Wilkinson got the credit for devising dazzle, and he alone published a book about his experiences, *A Brush with Life*, which helped cement his legacy. But when I saw a photograph in his book showing some of the young women who worked at the dazzle studio in London, I knew I needed to mention them.

I had wrongly assumed that at that time in history, Wilkinson's staff would have been all male, and I didn't want my readers to make the same mistake.

Other than Eva Mackenzie, who later became Mrs. Wilkinson, I don't know the names of these women. But I do know that they played an important part in the story of dazzle ships, just as that photo (which you'll see when you turn the page) played an important part in my telling of it.

While photographs can be enormously helpful, they can sometimes conceal information. For example, black-and-white photos of dazzle ships at sea don't convey the array of colors used in those designs.

Just as we need to consider what a photo might not show, we should also give some thought to how photos—and all our research finds—contrast with the images and stories we already had in mind. Research done right does not merely confirm what you expect to see—it will show things you had not anticipated. The more you research, the more surprises you'll find, and that's exciting. For me, the risk of information overload is always more than worth it.

ILLUSTRATOR'S NOTE

For me, choosing art as a career was all about passion, but I sometimes wonder how meaningful art truly is. While illustrating *Dazzle Ships*, I found myself thinking about this question in new ways.

I am not a writer, so I'd like to borrow some wise words from author, illustrator, and pilot Antoine de Saint-Exupéry. He said, "The theoretician believes in logic and believes that he despises dreams, intuition, and poetry. He does not recognize that these three fairies have only disguised themselves in order to dazzle him. . . . He does not know that he owes his greatest discoveries to them."

I agreed to take on this project because I was intrigued by the story and I like to draw oceans, patterns, and ships. As I worked on the illustrations, I reflected on the many different ways that art is essential in our lives—whether it's part of a military strategy or part of a picture book that opens readers' eyes to something they hadn't considered before.

If you look closely, you may notice a small symbol on each piece of art in this book that's reminiscent of a seal you might find in traditional East Asian artwork. It is similar to the Chinese character for my middle name, and if you turn it sideways, you'll see it's my first name. I include it in all of my work as an acknowledgment of my heritage—I was born in China and raised in Hong Kong.

Finally, I want to give a shout-out to the team that made this book possible. Thank you to my art director Danielle Carnito and editor Carol Hinz for fully understanding (and tolerating) the "personal" aspect of art making—you have been nothing but patient with me throughout this journey. I am very grateful to be working with you on my debut picture book. Thank you my dear agent Gail Gaynin: you are a perfect hybrid of business partner, cheerleader, and therapist.

TIMELINE

AUGUST 1914: Following the assassination of Archduke Franz Ferdinand and Germany's declaration of war on Russia, Belgium, and France, Britain declares war on Germany.

SEPTEMBER 1914: German submarine *U-9* torpedoes and sinks Royal Navy ships *Aboukir*, *Cressy*, and *Hogue*, killing 1,459 people.

FEBRUARY 1915: Germany promises to attack any merchant vessel belonging to Britain or its allies, including ships carrying civilians.

MARCH 1915: Britain imposes a blockade on ships heading for German ports. No ships carrying food or other goods to Germany are to be allowed through.

MAY 1915: *U-20* sinks the *Lusitania*, a British ship carrying both civilians and munitions. The attack kills about 1,200 people, including more than 120 Americans.

SEPTEMBER 1915: Under pressure from the United States, Germany restricts its use of submarines.

FEBRUARY 1917: Germany—which is facing food shortages and desperate for an advantage against Britain—resumes unrestricted submarine warfare.

APRIL 1917: The United States enters the war against Germany. As Britain loses dozens of ships to U-boat attacks each week, British leaders confront the possibility of their people's starvation. Norman Wilkinson—a painter-turned-Royal Naval Volunteer Reserve lieutenant-commander—gets the idea to paint merchant ships so that they appear distorted to submarine crews.

MID-1917: Wilkinson's approach becomes known as dazzle. The HMS *Industry* becomes the first dazzle-painted ship. Artists, designers, and model makers begin working at Burlington House in London to come up with dazzle patterns.

OCTOBER 1917: King George V visits the dazzle studios at Burlington House. The British government orders that all merchant ships receive unique dazzle designs.

Wilkinson during World War I. In his book *A Brush with Life*, he said, "Now, ideas, inventions, and original thoughts come to one in various ways. Some are well thought out, others come to one in a moment."

EARLY 1918: Wilkinson meets with US assistant secretary of the navy—and future president—Franklin D. Roosevelt. Soon after, the United States begins using dazzle on both merchant ships and warships.

SUMMER 1918: At ports around England, dazzle painting continues. In Liverpool alone, about 120 workers are involved in efforts to paint dazzle designs onto ships at dock. In New York, the Women's Reserve Camouflage Corps applies attention-getting dazzle overnight to a battleship-shaped recruiting station.

OCTOBER 1918: The count of dazzle-painted British merchant ships hits 2,719, plus another 251 dazzled warships.

NOVEMBER 1918: The war ends with Germany's new government signing an armistice with the Allies. More than 1,200 US vessels have been painted with dazzle designs.

British patrol boat HMS *Kildangan* displays its dazzle in 1918.

Top: The mock ship USS *Recruit*, which stood in New York City's Union Square and was used as a naval recruiting station, got dazzled overnight in 1918.

Bottom: Members of Wilkinson's team are at work in their studio at the Royal Academy in London's Burlington House.

FOR FURTHER READING

On the subject of human-made camouflage, I believe there is no better source for information than artist, designer, historian, and teacher Roy R. Behrens. His website, camoupedia.blogspot.com, is a well-organized visual treat with links to lots of additional sources of information about camouflage, including Behrens's own books on the topic.

For additional reading about other aspects of the dazzle ships story, I recommend these books:

DiSpezio, Michael A. *Optical Illusion Magic: Visual Tricks & Amusements*. New York: Sterling, 1999.

Freedman, Russell. *The War to End All Wars: World War I*. Boston: Clarion Books, 2010.

Grant, R. G. *World War I: The Definitive Visual History; From Sarajevo to Versailles*. New York: DK, 2014.

Mallard, Neil. *Submarine*. New York: DK, 2003.

Preston, Diana. *Remember the* Lusitania*!* New York: Walker, 2003.

Seckel, Al. *The Ultimate Book of Optical Illusions*. New York: Sterling, 2006.

Swanson, Jennifer. *How Submarines Work*. Illustrated by Glen Mullaly. Mankato, MN: Child's World, 2012.

YOU CAN FIND THE COMPLETE BIBLIOGRAPHY OF SOURCES CONSULTED AT
HTTP://WWW.CHRISBARTON.INFO/BOOKS/DAZZLE.HTML.

Text copyright © 2017 by Chris Barton
Illustrations copyright © 2017 by Victo Ngai

All rights reserved. International copyright secured. No part of this book may be reproduced, stored in
a retrieval system, or transmitted in any form or by any means—electronic, mechanical, photocopying,
recording, or otherwise—without the prior written permission of Lerner Publishing Group, Inc., except for
the inclusion of brief quotations in an acknowledged review.

Millbrook Press
A division of Lerner Publishing Group, Inc.
241 First Avenue North
Minneapolis, MN 55401 USA

For reading levels and more information, look up this title at www.lernerbooks.com.

The images in this book are used with the permission of: Imperial War Museum, London, p. 34; National
Archives (165-WW-599G-9), p. 35 (top); © Royal Academy of Arts, London, p. 35 (middle); © IWM/Getty
Images, p. 35 (bottom).

Designed by Danielle Carnito.
The illustrations in this book were created using mixed analog and digital media.
Main body text set in Gill Sans Standard 14/17.5. Typeface provided by Monotype Typography.
Gill Sans was designed by Eric Gill (1882–1940), an English sculptor, type designer, and printmaker. The
typeface was derived from the lettering created for the London Underground by designer Edward Johnston
in 1916—a project with which Gill had assisted in its early stages. After he painted the façade of a bookshop
in Bristol, England, in all capital letters, Gill was commissioned to create a font that could compete with the
clean, sans serif German fonts being produced at the time. Gill Sans was released as titling capitals in 1928,
with lowercase letters following shortly after.

Library of Congress Cataloging-in-Publication Data

Names: Barton, Chris, author. | Ngai, Victo, 1988– illustrator.
Title: Dazzle ships : World War I and the art of confusion / Chris Barton ; illustrated by Victo Ngai.
Other titles: World War I and the art of confusion
Description: Minnneapolis : Millbrook Press, [2017] | Includes bibliographical references. | Audience:
    Grades K–3.
Identifiers: LCCN 2016045544 (print) | LCCN 2016045654 (ebook) | ISBN 9781512410143 (library binding :
    alk. paper) | ISBN 9781512451108 (eb pdf)
Subjects: LCSH: Warships—Great Britain—Juvenile literature. | Warships—Camouflage—Juvenile
    literature. | World War, 1914–1918—Camouflage—Juvenile literature. | World War, 1914–1918—Art
    and the war—Juvenile literature.
Classification: LCC V215 .B34 2017 (print) | LCC V215 (ebook) | DDC 940.4/5941—dc23

LC record available at https://lccn.loc.gov/2016045544

Manufactured in the United States of America
5-47442-21261-3/20/2019